Treasure Island

Robert Louis Stevenson

Adapted by Alan MacDonald

Illustrated by Martin Cottam

About the Author

ROBERT LOUIS STEVENSON

1850–1894

Robert Louis Stevenson was born in Edinburgh and trained as a lawyer. He wrote some plays, and books about his travels in France and Belgium, but his first full-length story was *Treasure Island*.

He got the idea for the story from a map his stepson, Lloyd, had drawn when they were on holiday. Between them they invented names for the places on the island. That imaginary island inspired Stevenson to write *Treasure Island*.

Long John Silver was Stevenson's favourite character in *Treasure Island* – years later, he wrote that he still admired 'that smooth and formidable character'.

This adaptation of *Treasure Island* uses some words which may be unfamiliar – either because they are old, or because they are connected to ships and sailing.

To find the meanings of these words, look in the Glosssary on page 119.

CHAPTER I

The Old Sea Dog

I remember him as if it were yesterday. A tall nut-brown man with broken nails and a white scar across one cheek. He rapped on the door of the Admiral Benbow inn and called for a glass of rum. The inn belonged to my father and I – Jim Hawkins – helped to serve in the parlour.

'This is a handy spot,' said the stranger. 'Do you get many visitors?'

'Not many,' my father told him regretfully.

'Well then,' he said, 'this is the place for me. I'm a plain man, rum and bacon and eggs is all I want, and the cliffs here to watch out for ships.'

He told us to call him 'captain' and had his chest carried upstairs to his room.

All day the captain would walk the cliffs, looking through his brass telescope. In the evenings he'd sit in a corner by the fire and drink strong rum. Every day when he came back from his walk he'd ask the same question: 'Have any seafaring men been by today?' He promised me a silver fourpence once a month if I'd keep my eyes open 'for a sea-faring man with one leg'. The moment he appeared I was to run and tell the captain. How that one-legged man haunted my dreams! On stormy nights, when the wind shook the house, he would chase me through my nightmares, leaping and running with terrible speed.

The captain stayed on week after week, and then month after month. He never paid his bill and my father was too scared of him to ask for the money.

Everyone was afraid of the captain. In the evenings, when he'd drunk too much rum he would sit and sing his wild, old sea-songs.

> 'Fifteen men on the dead man's chest
> Yo-ho-ho and a bottle of rum!
> Drink and the devil had gone for the rest
> Yo-ho-ho and a bottle of rum!'

Everyone at the inn joined in the singing on the captain's orders. Sometimes he would tell stories of the sea – grim stories about hanging and walking the plank and terrible storms. No one was allowed to leave the inn until he'd drunk himself sleepy and rolled off to bed.

Only one man ever spoke back to him and that was Dr Livesey. The doctor was in the parlour at the time, talking to old Taylor the gardener. Suddenly the captain banged on the table for silence. Everyone stopped talking at once – except for Dr Livesey.

'Silence there between decks!' growled the captain.

'Are you talking to me?' replied the doctor coolly. 'If

you go on drinking rum like that, the world will soon be rid of a dirty scoundrel.'

The captain instantly flew into a rage. He opened his sailor's knife and threatened to pin the doctor to the wall. The doctor didn't even turn round in his chair.

'If you don't put that knife away, I'll have you arrested,' he said. 'I am a magistrate as well as a doctor and I'll be keeping a close eye on a rogue like you.'

Soon after that Dr Livesey left, but the captain was quiet that evening and for many evenings afterwards.

CHAPTER 2

Black Dog

Not long afterwards the first stranger came to the inn looking for the captain.

My mother was upstairs with my father who was very ill. The captain was out walking the cliffs as usual and I was busy getting his breakfast. The door opened and in walked a pale, greasy man with two fingers missing from his left hand. He wore a cutlass at his belt though he didn't look like much of a fighter.

'Come here, sonny,' he said to me. 'Is my mate Bill staying here? He has a scar on one cheek.'

I told him the captain was out walking. The stranger

waited just inside the door, peering round the corner like a cat waiting for a mouse. I didn't trust him but there was little I could do.

At last the captain walked in.

'Bill,' said the stranger, in a voice that I thought he tried to make bold and strong.

The captain spun round and all the colour drained from his face. He looked as if he was staring at a ghost.

'Come, Bill, you know me, your old shipmate.'

The captain gave a kind of gasp. 'Black Dog!' he said.

Black Dog ordered a glass of rum and the two men sat

talking in low voices. I brought the drink and left them together. I tried my best to listen from the bar but for a long time, I could only hear a low muttering. Then voices were raised and the captain cried out, 'No, no, no! If it comes to hanging, we all hang, say I.'

Then there was a tremendous explosion of noise. The chair and the table crashed over, there was the clash of steel blades and a cry of pain. The next minute I saw Black Dog running out with the captain chasing him. Black Dog had blood streaming from his shoulder.

The captain staggered back into the house. 'Jim!' he called to me. 'Rum.' He clutched at the wall to stop himself falling.

'Are you hurt?' I asked.

'Rum,' he repeated. 'I must get away from here. Rum, rum!'

I ran to fetch it but while I was gone I heard a loud fall in the parlour.

When I returned I found the captain lying on the floor. He was breathing heavily and his face had turned a deathly colour. My mother came running downstairs, but neither of us knew what to do. Luckily at that moment, Dr Livesey arrived to visit my father.

'Doctor! Is he wounded?' I asked.

'Wounded? Fiddlesticks!' said the doctor. 'The man has had a stroke, just as I warned him. He'll kill himself if he keeps on drinking rum.'

Between us we managed to get the captain up to bed where the doctor said he must stay for a week. If he had another stroke it would certainly be the death of him.

CHAPTER 3

The Black Spot

Later I went to the captain's room with some medicine. He seemed weak but also excited.

'Jim,' he said, 'you know I've always been good to you. Gave you a silver fourpence every month. You see how low I am. Bring me a glass of rum, won't you, matey?'

'But the doctor...' I began.

'Doctors is all swabs!' he interrupted. 'What do they know of a seaman's life? I lived on rum, I tell you. It's been meat and drink to me and if I don't get it now I'm nothing but a poor old wreck on the shore. I'll give you a golden guinea for a glass, Jim.'

He was getting more and more excited. I didn't want him to wake my father who was very sick that day, so I brought him the rum. He snatched it and drank it down greedily.

'Ay, ay, that's better,' he said. 'Now, how long did that doctor say I was to lie here in bed?'

'A week at least,' I answered.

'A week? By thunder, I can't do that! They'll have the black spot on me by then. They'll be getting news of me this very moment.'

As he spoke he tried to raise himself up, leaning hard on me. But he was too weak and sank back on the bed.

'Jim,' he said after a while, 'you saw that seafaring man today?'

'Black Dog?' I asked.

'Ah, Black Dog. He's a bad 'un, but there's worse who sent him. It's my old sea-chest they're after, Jim. If I can't get away, you jump on a horse and go to that doctor and tell him to bring help to the inn. Tell him he can arrest old Flint's crew, all that's left of them. I was Flint's mate and I'm the only one that knows the place. He gave it to me when he lay dying, just like *I* am now.'

'But what is the Black Spot, captain?' I asked.

'That's the sign they gives you when they're coming for you, mate.'

His voice was getting weaker but he rambled on for a while until I gave him his medicine.

Perhaps I should have gone to the doctor then and told him the whole story. But I didn't get a chance – that evening my father died very suddenly. With all the arrangements for the funeral and my own sad thoughts, I soon forgot all about the captain.

The next morning he managed to get downstairs. He ate little but helped himself to more rum from the bar.

The day after the funeral was a cold foggy morning. I was standing by the door thinking about my poor father, when I saw someone coming up the hill. He tapped in front of himself with a stick, so I guessed he was blind. Bent over, he wore a huge old tattered sea-cloak that made him look like a strange bird.

'Will any kind friend tell a poor old blind man where he is?' he cried in an odd sing-song voice.

'You are at the Admiral Benbow inn,' I answered.

'Give me your hand, my kind young friend, and lead me in,' he said.

The moment he had my hand, he gripped it like iron.

'Now, boy,' he said, 'take me in to the captain, or I'll break your arm.'

I never heard a voice so cruel or cold as that blind man's. I was more terrified of him than the captain himself.

I led him inside, and spoke the words he told me to say.

'Look, here's a friend for you, Bill.'

The poor captain raised his eyes and turned deathly pale.

'Now, Bill, sit where you are,' said the blind man. 'Business is business. Hold out your left hand. Boy, bring it near to me.'

We both obeyed and I saw him pass something into the captain's hand.

'And now that's done,' said the blind man. He suddenly let go of me and darted out of the door with surprising speed.

It was some time before the captain or I moved or spoke. Then the captain drew in his hand and looked at what lay in it.

'Ten o clock!' he cried. 'Six hours. We'll beat them yet,' and he sprang to his feet.

Even as he did, he clutched at his throat and stood

swaying for a moment. Then with a peculiar sound he fell face down on the floor.

I called for my mother but there was nothing she could do. The captain was dead, killed by a second stroke just as Dr Livesey had predicted. Though I'd never liked him, I burst into tears. It was the second death under our roof in a few days.

CHAPTER 4

The Sea-Chest

It didn't take long to tell my mother what I knew. We both realized that we were in great danger. At any hour the captain's desperate shipmates might arrive at our door. We were owed some of his money, but men like Black Dog wouldn't care much about that.

We ran to the village to get help. But our neighbours were all too terrified to help us try and defend the inn. The mention of Captain Flint's name filled them with terror. One lad offered to ride to Dr Livesey's but that was all the help we got.

My mother spoke angrily.

'Back we go then, Jim,' she said. 'If these chicken-hearted men won't help us, we'll go alone. We'll open the captain's chest and have the money he owes us, not a penny more or less.'

Back at the inn I bolted the door. The captain was where we'd left him, lying on the floor with eyes wide open. Close to his hand was a round piece of paper blackened on one side. On the other side were the words: 'You have till ten tonight.'

'Draw the blinds, Jim,' said my mother, 'and help me find the key to that chest.'

We searched his pockets, but only found a few coins, some tobacco and a pocket compass.

'Perhaps it's round his neck,' said my mother.

Biting my lip, I tore open his shirt. Sure enough there was the key, tied to a piece of string.

We hurried upstairs to the captain's room. My mother knelt over the old seaman's chest and turned the key in the lock. From inside came a strong smell of tobacco. At the very bottom we found a bundle tied up in oilcloth, and a bag that jingled with coins.

Counting the coins was a slow business but my mother insisted we take only what we were owed. We were half way through when I heard a sound that made my heart stop – the tap-tapping of a blind man's stick on the road. As I held my breath I heard the door-bolt being rattled downstairs. Then the tap-tap went away down the hill.

'Mother,' I said, 'we must get away before it's too late.'

I hid the oilcloth packet inside my jacket and we crept downstairs. Soon we were out of the door and into the night. The fog was beginning to clear and a full moon shone brightly. Already we could hear footsteps approaching and see a lantern coming up the hill. By good luck we managed to reach the little bridge over the stream. We slid quickly down the bank and hid underneath the arch. There we stayed, not daring to move, as the voices drew nearer and nearer.

CHAPTER 5

The Last of the Blind Man

After a while, my curiosity was too strong to resist. I crawled back up the bank and hid behind a bush where I could see the road to our door. I was just in time to watch our enemies arrive. There were seven or eight of them, running hard. Three of them ran hand in hand and I recognized the middle one as the blind man.

Finding the door open, four rushed into the inn. There was a pause, then a cry of surprise.

'Bill's dead!'

'Search him,' cried the blind man. 'The rest of you – upstairs and get the chest.'

Seconds later the window of the captain's room was thrown open. A man leaned out into the moonlight and shouted to the blind man below.

'Pew! Someone's been here before us. They've turned out the chest.'

'Is it there?' roared Pew.

'Gone,' replied the man.

'It's that boy and his mother. I wish I'd put his eyes out,' cried the blind man. 'Scatter, lads, and find them.'

Next came the sound of the inn being searched from

top to bottom. Furniture was thrown over, doors were kicked in and feet pounded up and down stairs. At last they reported that there was no sign of us. Just then I heard a whistle from the direction of the village. I guessed that it was a signal warning of danger.

'There's Dirk,' said one. 'We'll have to fly, mates.'

'Run, you fool?' cried Pew. 'Stay and look for that boy. You'd be as rich as kings if you could find it and you stand there dawdling.'

'Hang it, Pew, we've got the money, let's go,' grumbled one.

At that Pew flew into a rage and began striking out at them with his stick. This quarrel saved our lives, because soon we heard the sound of horses galloping towards us. The men heard it too and ran in every direction. In less than a minute the only one left on the road was Blind Pew. He tapped up and down in a panic, calling for his friends.

'Johnny! Black Dog! You won't leave old Pew behind, mates! Not old Pew!'

Just then the horses came over the hill and thundered down towards us. Pew ran away with a scream and slipped in a ditch. In a second he was up again and made another blind dash – but this time right into the path of one of the horses. His cry split the night. Then he fell by the road, stone dead.

I jumped to my feet and called to the riders. I

recognized the lad from the village who had gone for help. The other riders were customs men led by their officer, Mr Dance. I returned with him to the Admiral Benbow which we found in a terrible state.

'Well then, Hawkins, what do you think they were after? Money?' asked Mr Dance.

'No, sir, I think I have the thing in my jacket pocket,' I answered. 'To tell the truth I'd like to put it somewhere safe. I thought I'd give it to Dr Livesey.'

'Quite right,' he agreed. 'I'm going to call on him now and report to him what's happened. You can come with me if you like and tell him the whole story.'

CHAPTER 6

Captain Flint's Secret

Dr Livesey's maid told us that he was at Squire Trelawney's house. An hour later we were sitting in the squire's library in front of a bright fire.

Mr Dance told them the whole story and long before it was finished Squire Trelawney was striding about the room excitedly. He was a tall, broad-chested man with a red face. His eyebrows were very black which made him look short-tempered.

When Mr Dance had gone, the doctor turned to me.

19

'So, Jim, you have the thing they were after, have you?'

'Here it is, sir,' I said, handing him the oilskin packet.

'You've heard of this Flint, I suppose,' he asked the squire.

'Heard of him?' said the squire. 'He was the most bloodthirsty pirate that ever sailed.'

'Well then, what if this packet here is a clue to where Flint buried his treasure? Would it be worth something?'

'Worth something?' cried the squire. 'It would be worth enough for me to hire a ship in Bristol and take you and Hawkins here along to find the treasure.'

Dr Livesey smiled and opened the package on the table. Out fell a map of an island nine miles long. On one side of the island was a hill marked 'Spy Glass Hill'. What interested us most were three crosses in red ink. Next to one was written neatly: 'Bulk of Treasure Here.'

There was no doubt: we were looking at Captain Flint's treasure map.

Over on the back there was more in the same handwriting.

> *Tall tree, Spy Glass shoulder, bearing a point to the N of N.N.E.*
> *Skeleton Island E.S.E and by E. Ten feet.*
> *The silver bar is in the north pit. You can find it by the*

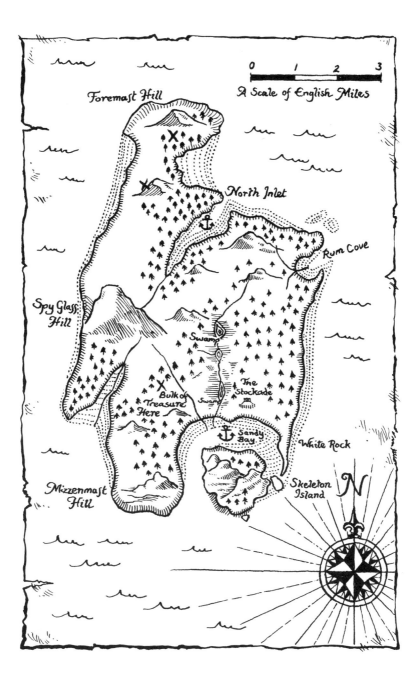

slope of the east hill, ten fathoms south of the black crag with the face on it. The arms are easily found in the sand hill, N point of North Inlet cape, bearing E and a quarter N.

That was all, but it was enough to convince the squire that we were looking at the key to Flint's treasure.

'Livesey,' he said, 'tomorrow I will go to Bristol and in three weeks' time, we'll have the best ship and the finest crew in England. Hawkins shall come along as cabin-boy. You will be our ship's doctor. We'll take my own men, Redruth, Hunter and Joyce. With fair winds and this map we'll find the treasure and live like kings for the rest of our lives.'

'Trelawney, I'll go with you,' said the doctor. 'I'm sure Jim will too. There's only one man I'm afraid of.'

'Who?' asked the squire. 'Name the dog!'

'You,' replied the doctor, 'because you cannot hold your tongue. We aren't the only ones who know about this map. These men who raided the inn tonight were bold, desperate fellows and they mean to have this treasure. We must be careful and not breathe a word of this map to anyone.'

'Livesey, you're right as always,' said the squire. 'I shall be silent as the grave.'

CHAPTER 7

I Go to Bristol

While Squire Trelawney was in Bristol, I stayed on at the Hall in case the pirates returned to the Admiral Benbow to look for the map.

One fine day a letter arrived for Dr Livesey. There was a note on the envelope saying: 'In the doctor's absence, to be opened by Jim Hawkins.' As I hoped, it contained news from the squire in Bristol.

Old Anchor Inn, Bristol
March 1st

Dear Livesey

The ship is bought and lies at anchor ready for sea. You never imagined a sweeter craft and her name is Hispaniola.

Finding the ship was no trouble but a crew was another matter, until I had a stroke of fortune. One morning on the dock I ran into an old sailor who runs an inn nearby. He knows all the seamen in Bristol and wanted a job as ship's cook to smell the salt of the sea again. Long John Silver is his name and he lost one leg serving his country in the navy. He soon helped me to find a crew who are some of the toughest old salts you can imagine.

They're not pretty to look at but by their faces they are bold and brave fellows.

I am itching to weigh anchor and get to sea. Let young Hawkins go and see his mother with my gamekeeper Redruth to watch over him. Then both come full speed to Bristol.

John Trelawney

The next day I said goodbye to my mother and the cove where I had lived since I was born. We took the night mail coach to Bristol and arrived the next morning. At a large inn we met Squire Trelawney, all dressed up in blue like a naval officer.

'Here you are,' he cried, 'and the doctor came last night from London. Our ship's company is complete.'

'Oh, sir, when do we sail?' I cried.

'Sail?' said he. 'We sail tomorrow!'

CHAPTER 8

At the Sign of the Spy Glass

After breakfast the squire gave me a note to take to Long John Silver at the Spy Glass inn. I soon found the place under a newly painted sign of a large brass telescope. Inside, the room was full of seamen who talked so loudly that I hung outside the door, scared to enter.

Just then a man came out of a side room. I guessed he was Long John Silver. He had only one good leg but he got around at surprising speed on a crutch, hopping about on it like a bird. He was tall and strong with a face as big as a ham. It was an intelligent face and he always seemed to be cheerful. As he moved among the tables he whistled and stopped to share a joke with his customers. I'd been worrying that Silver might be the one-legged man I'd been warned of at the Admiral Benbow. But one look at this clean and smiling landlord told me he was no pirate like Blind Pew or Black Dog.

I plucked up courage and went inside the inn.

'Mr Silver, sir?' I asked, holding out my note.

'Yes, my lad. And who may you be?' he said.

Then, as he saw the squire's letter, his expression changed.

'Oh,' he said, quite loudly. 'So you are our new cabin-boy? Very pleased I am to meet you.'

Just then one of the customers rose suddenly and darted out of the door. His haste caught my attention and I recognized him at once.

'Stop him!' I cried. 'It's Black Dog!'

'I don't care two pennies who he is,' answered Silver, 'but he hasn't paid for his drink. Harry, run and catch him!'

One of the others who was near the door went off in pursuit.

'Who did you say he was?' asked Silver. 'Black what?'

'Dog, sir,' I said. 'Hasn't Mr Trelawney told you about the pirates? He was one of them!'

'So?' cried Silver. 'One of those swabs, was he? In my house. Was you drinking with him, Morgan? Step over here.'

The man called Morgan, an old grey-haired sailor, came forward obediently.

'Now, Morgan,' said Long John sternly, 'you never clapped eyes on that Black Dog before, did you now?'

'Not I, sir,' said Morgan with a salute.

'You didn't know his name, did you?'

'No, sir.'

'It's just as well for you, Tom Morgan. If I thought you was mixed up with that kind of fellow, you'd never set foot in my house again.'

As Morgan rolled back to his seat, Silver whispered to me. 'He's an honest man, Morgan, only stupid. Now this Black Dog. Come to think of it, *I've* seen the swab before. He used to come in here with a blind beggar.'

'That's him. The blind man!' I said. 'His name was Pew!'

'It was!' cried Silver, now quite excited. 'Well, I hope we catch this Black Dog. That will be good news for Cap'n Trelawney.'

But just then the man called Harry came back out of breath and admitted he had lost Black Dog in the crowd. Silver scolded him badly and then took me on one side.

'See here now, Hawkins, this looks bad for me. What's Captain Trelawney to think? Here I find this dog sitting in my own house, drinking my own rum. And then he runs off and gets clean away. You'll stand up for me with the captain, won't you? You're only a lad but you're as smart as paint, I see that when you first came in.'

Since finding Black Dog at the inn, I'd watched the cook closely, but by now I would have swom to the innocence of Long John Silver.

We went straight to the squire to report what had happened. Long John told the story, missing out nothing from first to last. 'That was how it were, now weren't it,

Hawkins?' he would say to me and I was always able to back him up.

The squire and the doctor regretted that Black Dog had got away but told Silver that he couldn't be blamed.

When he had gone, Dr Livesey said, 'Well, I don't put much faith in your choices, Trelawney, but that Silver is a good man.' He turned to me. 'And now, Jim, it's time you came aboard the *Hispaniola*.'

CHAPTER 9

Powder and Arms

We rowed out to the ship in a small boat. As soon as we got down into the cabin, Captain Smollett asked to speak with us. The captain was a sharp-looking man, who seemed angry with everything on board.

'Well, Captain Smollett, what do you have to say? All shipshape and seaworthy?' asked the squire.

'Well, sir,' said the captain, 'I'm a plain-speaking man. I don't like this voyage, I don't like its purpose, and I don't like my crew. That's it, short and sweet.'

I could tell the squire was on the point of exploding, but Dr Livesey cut in.

'You say you don't like this voyage, sir. Why not?'

'The crew knows more about our voyage than I do. I don't call that fair, do you?'

'No,' said Dr Livesey. 'I do not.'

'Next,' said the captain, 'I find out we're going after treasure. Treasure is dangerous work. I don't like treasure voyages and I don't like it when the secret has been blabbed to every man aboard. I doubt if you gentlemen understand the risk you are taking.'

'And the crew?' asked the doctor. 'Aren't they good seamen?'

'I should have chosen them myself,' replied Captain Smollett.

'Well now, and what does this all add up to, captain?' asked the doctor. 'What do you want?'

'Very good,' said the captain. 'If you are set upon this voyage, take my advice. The crew are putting the powder and the arms in the bows. Have them brought back here to the cabin. Secondly, have your own people sleep here beside the cabin. And lastly, there's been too much blabbing of secrets already.'

'Agreed,' said the doctor. 'What have you heard?'

'That you have a map of an island, and that there's crosses on the map to show where the treasure is,' said the captain. To our dismay he went on to name the exact position of the island.

'I never told that to a soul!' exclaimed the squire.

The captain ignored this. 'Well, gentlemen,' he said. 'I don't know who has this map, and I wish it to be kept secret from me. Otherwise I ask you to let me resign.'

Dr Livesey nodded. 'You advise us to turn the cabin of the ship into a fortress. In other words you fear a mutiny, sir?'

'I don't say that. But as captain I'm responsible for the safety of every man Jack aboard this ship. I ask you to take certain steps, otherwise I resign my post. That's all.'

The squire blew out his cheeks and looked angry. 'Sir,

we've heard what you have to say and will do as you wish, but I think the worse of you.'

'That's as you please,' said the captain and took his leave.

'Trelawney,' said the doctor, 'I think you may have got two honest men aboard. That man and Silver.' The squire replied with a snort of disgust.

Later the crew were moving the powder to lodge it in the cabin when Silver came on board.

'So-ho, mates! What's this?' he asked.

'We're changing the powder, John,' answered one.

'My orders!' said the captain shortly. 'And you, ship's boy! Out of the way and get below with the cook to do some work. I'll have no favourites on my ship.'

I obeyed, but decided that I hated the captain deeply.

CHAPTER 10

The Voyage

All that night we were busy getting ready to set sail. Mr Blandly who had helped the squire buy the ship came to wish us a good voyage. It was agreed that if we weren't home by the end of August then he would send a rescue boat to look for us.

Finally, a little before dawn, we prepared to weigh the anchor.

The boatswain sounded his pipe and the crew manned the capstan bars.

'Now, John, sing us a song. The old one,' said one of the men to Silver.

'Ay ay, mates,' said Long John who was standing by. He sang out the words I knew so well.

> 'Fifteen men on the dead man's chest
> Yo-ho-ho and a bottle of rum!'

The men joined in and at the third 'ho!' pushed the capstan bars with all their might. Soon the anchor was up and hung dripping at the bow of the ship. The sails began to fill and the ship drew away from the docks. We had begun our voyage to Treasure Island!

The captain was forced to admit that he'd been wrong about the crew for they were all good seamen. As for me, I was often in the galley working with Long John Silver. He was always kind to me and showed me his parrot which he kept in a cage.

'This is Cap'n Flint, young Hawkins. I calls him after the famous pirate, don't I, Flint?'

And the parrot would reply, 'Pieces of eight! Pieces of eight! Pieces of eight!'

'That bird is two hundred years old, Hawkins,' said Silver, 'and he's seen more wickedness than the devil himself.'

All the crew respected and even obeyed Silver whom they called Barbecue. 'He's no common man, Barbecue,' one of the men told me. 'He had schooling when he was young and can speak like a book. As for brave? – I seen him tackle four men unarmed and knock their heads together.'

The days passed quickly and the *Hispaniola* proved to be a good ship. The voyage was long and uneventful until the last day. It was then I had the lucky accident which was to save all our lives.

We were very near the island and sailing in a quiet sea with a steady breeze. It was after sundown when I finished my work. Feeling hungry, I decided to get myself an apple from the barrel on deck. The only fruit was at the bottom of the apple barrel, so I had to climb right inside. Just then a heavy man sat down and leaned his shoulders against the barrel. I was about to come out when he began to speak and I recognized Silver's voice. Before I had heard a dozen words I realized that the life of every honest man aboard depended on me alone.

What I Heard in the Apple Barrel

'No,' said Silver. 'Flint was the captain, not I. What a battle that was! In the same broadside I lost my leg, and old Pew lost his eyes. Ay, I've seen Flint's ship awash with red blood and fit to sink with gold.'

'Ah, he was the cream of the crop, was Flint,' said the other. I recognized his voice as Dick, the youngest seaman on board.

'He's dead now,' said Silver. 'And Blind Pew and Billy Bones too. And them that's left of Flint's crew are aboard this ship. That's why I wanted to have this talk with you. You're young but you're smart as paint, I see that when I first set eyes on you. You could be a gentleman of fortune like myself. We live rough, but we eat and drink like fighting cocks with hundreds of pounds in our pocket. Are you with us?'

'I am and here's my hand on it,' said Dick and I felt the barrel move as the two men shook hands.

Soon a third man strolled up and sat down by Silver.

'Dick is with us,' said Silver.

'Ay, he's no fool, is Dick,' agreed the other, whose voice betrayed him as Israel Hands, the coxswain. Hands spat on the deck. 'But look here, what I want to know is how long are we going to take orders from that Captain Smollett? He's crossed me once too often, by thunder.'

'Israel,' said Silver, 'you'll work hard and you'll speak soft until I give the word, my son.'

'All right, but what I say is, when?' growled the coxswain.

'I'll tell you when: the last moment, that's when. Here's this doctor and squire with a map – I don't know where it is, do I? I mean them to find the treasure and help us to get it aboard before we strike.'

'And what do we do with them then?' asked Israel.

'Well, what do you think? Put 'em ashore and leave 'em? Or cut 'em down like so much pork?'

'Billy was the man for that,' said Israel. 'Dead men don't bite, says he.'

'Right you are,' said Silver. 'I'm quite the gentleman but when it comes down to business, duty is duty, mates. I say we kill them.'

'John, you're a man,' said Hands.

'Only one thing I claim and that's Trelawney,' said Silver. 'I'll wring his fat neck with my bare hands.' Then he added, 'Dick, be a sweet lad and get me an apple from the barrel.'

You can imagine the terror I felt. I would have leaped out of the barrel and run for it, if I hadn't been frozen with fear. I heard Dick begin to rise but then Hands' voice stopped him.

'Never mind that, John. Let's have a round of the rum.'

'Dick, I trust you,' said Silver. 'There's the key. Go and bring us up a jug.'

Dick was gone a little while but in that time I gathered some important news. It seemed that not all the crew were with the pirates. 'Not another man'll join,' said Hands. It gave me a little hope, but I was still wondering how I was going to get out of the apple barrel alive. Just then my thoughts were interrupted by the cry of the look-out.

'Land-ho!'

CHAPTER 12

Council of War

There was a great rush of feet across the deck. While everyone was eager to catch a glimpse of the island, I slipped out of the apple barrel. I joined Hunter and Dr Livesey at the bow of the ship. In the moonlight we could see two low hills, about two miles apart. Rising between them was a third higher hill with its top buried in the fog.

'Has any one of you ever seen that land ahead?' asked the captain.

'I have, sir,' said Silver. 'That's Skeleton Island. We took on water there once, when I was ship's cook on a trading ship. It were a haunt for pirates once, I'm told. That hill – the big one – they calls the Spy Glass by reason of it being a look-out point.'

'I have a chart here,' said Captain Smollett. 'Is this the place?'

Long John's eyes burned in his head as he took the map. By the newness of the paper, I knew he'd be disappointed. It was a copy of the real map, with every detail except the three crosses which showed where the treasure was buried.

Silver managed to hide his annoyance. 'Yes, sir, this is the place. And very prettily drawn out. Who might have done that I wonder?'

'Thank you, my man. I may ask your help later to steer us into anchorage,' said Captain Smollett.

I watched all this in a dream, for my head was still full of what I'd heard in the apple barrel. Somehow I had to get a message to Captain Smollett or Dr Livesey without raising suspicion. While I was trying to think of a plan, Dr Livesey called me over to fetch his pipe from the cabin. I took my chance and whispered: 'Doctor, get the captain and the squire down to the cabin, then send for me on some errand. I have terrible news.'

'Thank you, Jim, that's all I wanted to know,' he said loudly as if he'd asked me some question. Dr Livesey spoke with the other two and I could tell they had got my message. A short time after, all hands were called on deck.

Captain Smollett addressed them. 'My lads, this land we've sighted is the island we have been sailing for. Every man on board has done his duty well and rum will be served to all of you. The squire, the doctor and I are going below to drink your health.'

A hearty cheer was raised for Captain Smollett. It was so willing that it was hard to believe these men were really plotting to murder us.

The three gentlemen went below. Soon after, I received a message that I was wanted in the cabin. The doctor was smoking his pipe and had his wig on his lap, which I knew meant he was worried.

'Now, Hawkins, you have something to tell us. Speak up,' said the squire.

I told them the whole tale, with all the details of what Silver and the others had said. All three listened in silence until I had finished.

'Jim,' said Dr Livesey, 'take a seat.'

They sat me down at the table and poured me a glass of wine. Each of them drank my health and praised me for my luck and courage.

'Now, captain,' said the squire. 'I admit you were right and I was wrong. I have been a fool.'

'No more than I,' said the captain. 'If this crew has mutiny in mind they've kept it hidden well.'

'That's Silver,' said the doctor. 'A very remarkable man.'

'He'd look remarkably well hanging from a rope,' replied the captain. 'But this talk gets us nowhere. We must work out a plan of action. Firstly, it's too late to turn back, that's clear. They would rise against us at once. Secondly, we have time on our side, at least until the treasure is found. Third point, we know some of the crew are honest. With the squire's three men and ourselves that makes seven, counting Hawkins. We must carry on as if nothing's changed and keep our eyes and ears open. Until we know which of the crew are on our side, we cannot come to blows.'

The doctor looked at me. 'Jim here can help us most. He can move among the men and he has a sharp pair of ears.'

I nodded but inside I felt scared and helpless. It was plain that our situation was desperate. We were seven and the pirates could count on as many as nineteen men. We would need more than good luck if we were ever going to see England again.

CHAPTER 13

How My Shore Adventure Began

The next morning the *Hispaniola* lay a half mile off the coast of the island. The woods were grey and the rocks stood above them in strange shapes. I could hear the surf thundering on the beach and the birds crying all around us. It made my heart sink. After such a long voyage, I hated the very sight of Treasure Island.

There was no wind. We had to tow the ship into a narrow passage to a safe anchorage behind Skeleton Island. The heat was sweltering and the men cursed and grumbled in the boats.

We anchored between the two islands. The drop of the anchor sent up clouds of birds wheeling and crying over the woods. There was a foul, stagnant smell in the air. I saw the doctor sniffing it like someone tasting a bad egg.

'I don't know about treasure,' he said, 'but I'd wager there's fever here.'

The crew's mood didn't improve once they were back on the ship. They lay around the deck muttering in low voices. Every order was received with a black look. It was plain that mutiny hung over us like a thundercloud. Long

John saw it too and tried his best to cover the men's dangerous mood. He kept up one song after another and sprang to obey every order with a cheery 'Ay ay, sir.'

Later in the cabin we discussed our situation.

Captain Smollett looked grim. 'If I risk another order, we'll have the whole crew up in arms against us. There's only one man we can rely on.'

'And who is that?' asked the squire.

'Silver,' replied the captain. 'You saw how he's behaving. He's anxious as we are to prevent the men taking over the ship now. He wants them to wait till he has his hands on the treasure. If he had the chance I believe he could talk the men out of this mood. Let's allow the crew an afternoon ashore. You mark my words, Silver will bring them back as gentle as lambs.'

We all agreed to the captain's plan. All the same we armed our trusted men with loaded pistols just in case. The captain then went on deck to address the men.

'Lads, we've had a hot day's work and we're all tired. Some time ashore will do us all a power of good. The boats are still in the water. Take them and have an afternoon ashore. I'll fire the gun half an hour before sundown for you to return.'

At this news, the men came out of their sulk and gave a loud cheer. I believe the silly fools thought they'd trip over the treasure as soon as they went ashore.

The captain kept out of the way and left Silver to arrange the shore party. To anyone watching it was clear that he was the true captain and they were his crew.

At last the shore party was ready. Thirteen were going to the island with Silver while six were to stay on board.

At this point an idea came to me. If Silver was leaving six men to watch the ship I was no use on board. On the other hand, if I went ashore I might learn something useful. Just as one of the boats shoved off, I slipped over the side and into it.

'Is that you, Jim? Keep your head down,' said one of the men.

Silver looked up sharply and called out, 'Is that young Hawkins?'

From that moment I regretted what I'd done. I'd acted without thinking and landed myself in great danger. But it was too late to go back now.

The boat I was in reached the shore first. Before anyone could stop me, I leapt out and ran into the woods.

I could hear Silver shouting behind me, 'Jim! Jim!' But I paid no attention. I ran and ducked under branches, till I was out of earshot.

CHAPTER 14

The First Blow is Struck

For the first time I felt the excitement of having an island to explore. I had given Long John and his crew the slip and there was no one to give me orders. I walked among strange twisted trees like oaks. The marsh steamed in the sunshine and Spy Glass Hill loomed up ahead of me.

All at once a flock of wild ducks flew up and I heard voices. Afraid, I crawled under one of the large trees.

From my hiding place I saw two men come into view. One was Silver and the other was a seaman called Tom. Silver had pushed back his hat and his big smooth face glowed in the sun.

'Mate,' he said, 'if I hadn't took such a liking to you, I wouldn't be giving you this warning. I'm only speaking to save your neck. If the others knew, they'd kill me.'

Tom's voice shook as he answered. 'Silver, you're old and you're honest. You wouldn't be led into mutiny by swabs like that? Not you! If I turn against my duty …'

All of a sudden a noise came from far out in the marsh: a cry of anger followed by another sound – a horrible, drawn-out scream. The rocks echoed with the sound and the marsh birds rose, beating their wings in the air.

Tom had heard it too.

'John! What was that?' he said.

'That?' Silver was smiling. 'Oh, I reckon that be Alan.'

Tom swung round on him. 'Alan! Then God rest his soul. And as for you, John Silver, you're no mate of mine. I won't join your gang of cutthroats. You've killed Alan and you'll have to kill me too.'

With those brave words, Tom turned his back on Silver and walked away. That was a mistake. With a cry of rage, Silver grabbed a branch and whipped out his crutch. He sent it hurtling through the air like a missile. It struck Tom a stunning blow between the shoulders and he fell forward with a gasp. Whether he was dead or not I couldn't tell, but Silver didn't wait to see. In a second he was on Tom with his knife and stabbed him in the back.

Sick with fear, I began to crawl away from that place as quickly as I could. Behind me I could hear Silver blow a blast on a whistle, and the answering shouts of his men. As soon as I was clear of the place, I ran as I'd never run before. I didn't care where I was going, as long as it was away from those murderers.

As I ran, my fear grew stronger each minute. What was I to do now? At sundown how could I go back to the boats and face those cold-blooded killers? Wouldn't the fact that I'd run away tell them I knew of their treachery? It was all over for me. I would never see my friends or my home again. I would either starve to death on the island or the pirates would catch me and wring my neck like a chicken.

At last I came to a part of the island where there were tall pine trees. Here a new danger brought me to a halt and set my heart racing.

CHAPTER 15

The Man of the Island

I saw something move behind the trees. Was it a man or a bear? I couldn't tell. It was dark and shaggy and moved with great speed.

I stopped, trying to think what to do. I was cut off on both sides. Behind me the murderers, ahead of me the thing in the trees. Wherever I went it followed me, darting from tree to tree like a deer. It ran like a man on two legs but it was bent over almost double. I began to think of what I'd heard about cannibals and was on the point of calling for help. Then I remembered my loaded pistol in my pocket. Taking courage, I walked straight towards the man of the island. He was hiding behind a tree-trunk. Seeing me, he came out and took a nervous step towards me. Then to my surprise he threw himself down on his knees.

'Who are you?' I asked.

'Ben Gunn,' he answered. His voice sounded like the scrape of a key in a rusty lock. 'Poor Ben Gunn I am, and I haven't spoken to a living soul for three long years.'

I had never seen such a ragged-looking beggar in my life. He was clothed with a patchwork of sail-cloth held together by buttons and bits of twig. His face and lips were burnt dark by the sun and his fair eyes gave him a startled expression.

'Three years?' I said. 'Were you shipwrecked?'

'No, mate – marooned,' he replied. 'They left me here three years ago and I've lived on goats and berries and oysters ever since. You don't happen to have a piece of cheese on you, do you?'

He was feeling in my pockets like an excited child.

'If ever I can get aboard again, you shall have cheese by the pound,' I said.

He looked me up and down. 'What do you call yourself, mate?'

'Jim,' I said.

'Jim, Jim,' he said, as if pleased with the sound. 'Now Jim, I'll tell you something.' He lowered his voice to a whisper. 'I'm rich. Rich! Rich! And I'll tell you what, I'll make a gentleman of you, Jim.'

I felt that, living alone on the island, the poor fellow must have gone half mad. He gripped my hand and held up his finger.

'Now, Jim, you tell me true: that ain't Flint's ship out there?'

'It's not,' I replied. 'Flint is dead. But there are some of Flint's men aboard, worse luck for us.'

'Not a man … with one … leg?' he gasped.

'Silver,' I said. 'He's the ringleader.'

He tightened his grip on my hand. 'If you was sent by Long John I'm as good as dead, mate.'

By now I was sure he was a friend – if a strange one. To calm his fears I told him the whole story of our voyage and the mutiny. When I'd finished he patted my head. 'You're a good lad, Jim, and you're in a tight spot, for sure. But you leave it to old Ben Gunn. This squire you talked of, is he a good man? If old Ben Gunn were to help you, would he get his share of the treasure and a passage home?'

'The squire is a gentleman,' I said. 'And besides, without a crew we'd need your help to sail the ship home.'

This seemed to put his mind at rest. We sat down and he began to tell me his story.

'I was in Flint's ship when he buried the treasure. Him and six strong seamen went ashore to bury it. They were gone a week. Then Flint came back in a boat by himself. Where's the other six, says you? Dead and buried. How he done it none of us knew. Long John and Billy Bones asked him where the treasure was. But Flint didn't answer and ordered us to put to sea.

'Well, three years ago I was on another ship and we came to this island. I knew it at once. "Boys," says I, "Flint's treasure lies here. Let's land and find it." The captain didn't like it, but the crew were with me. Twelve days we searched and found not a doubloon. Then they turned on old Ben Gunn. They left me here marooned with only a musket, a spade and a pick-axe for company. "You stay here," says they, "and find Flint's treasure yourself."

'Well, Jim, three years I've been here, rain and shine, night and day. Sometimes maybe I thinks of praying but most times I was busy with another matter.' He laughed to himself and added, 'You tell your squire, Gunn is a good man, he is.'

I shook my head. 'How can I talk to the squire when I can't even get aboard the ship?'

'Ah,' says he, 'I have a boat, made with my own hands. I keeps her by the big white rock on the beach. If it comes to the worst we can reach it after dark.' He broke off. 'Hi, what's that?'

For just at that moment the silence of the island was broken by cannon-fire.

'They've begun to fight!' I cried. 'Follow me!'

I ran towards the anchorage, all my fears forgotten. Ben Gunn trotted at my side, talking all the time in his wild way. The cannon-shot was followed by gun-fire. Then, a little way in front of me, I saw a Union Jack flutter in the air above a wood.

CHAPTER 16

The Story is Continued by Dr Livesey

How the Ship was Abandoned

It was about half past one when the two boats went ashore to the island. The captain, the squire and I talked things over in the cabin. If we'd had a breath of wind we would have attacked Silver's six men on board and made off with the ship. But there was no wind, and then Hunter told us the news that Jim Hawkins had gone ashore with the rest. With the men in such a dangerous mood, we feared for his life.

Waiting was a strain, so we decided Hunter and I

would go ashore in a boat to see what was happening. We rowed towards the island in the direction of the stockade that was marked on the map. Silver's men on the shore watched us go by, but stayed with their boats, as they'd been ordered.

Once on the island, I went to find the stockade. It was a log-house on the hill-top, surrounded by a fence, six feet high. It was big enough to hold twenty people and had loopholes to fire muskets from. Anyone with arms and ammunition could hold the place against a regiment. I made up my mind instantly to leave the *Hispaniola* and move to the stockade. Just as I was thinking that, I heard the cry of a dying man ring out across the island. My first thought was: 'Jim Hawkins is dead.'

It wasn't long before we were back on the *Hispaniola*. Everyone on board had heard that terrible cry. The squire was pale and one of Silver's men – Abraham Gray – looked just as shaken.

'There's a man who'll join us if he's steered in the right direction,' said the captain. 'He's not got the stomach for murder.'

I told my plan to the captain and we soon put it into action. Hunter brought the boat round to the stern of the ship where Joyce and I began loading her. We took muskets, powder, biscuits, pork and of course my medicine chest.

Meanwhile the squire and the captain stayed on deck, where they took Silver's men by surprise. Smollett called to the coxswain, 'Mr Hands, we are armed with pistols. If any one of you tries to signal to your friends, you're a dead man.'

By this time we had the boat loaded and Joyce, Hunter and I made for the shore as fast as we could row.

Our second trip caused a stir among Silver's men sitting on the shore. Before we were out of sight one of them went running off into the trees to find Long John. We landed out of their sight, and carried our supplies up to the stockade. I left Joyce and Hunter on guard with muskets while I rowed back to the *Hispaniola* alone.

The squire was waiting for me at the stern window. We loaded up the boat a second time. Now we had to hurry. We could hear shouts from the shore and knew that Silver's men had sounded the alarm. As Captain Smollett climbed into the boat he made one last appeal to Abraham Gray.

'Gray, do you hear me? I am leaving this boat and order you to follow your captain.'

There was no reply.

'Gray, I know you're a good man at heart. I give you thirty seconds to join me.'

There was a sound of a scuffle and Abraham Gray came running with a knife-cut on his cheek. He dropped into our boat and we shoved off from the ship.

We were clear of the *Hispaniola*, but by no means out of danger.

CHAPTER 17

The Boat's Last Trip

Our little boat was overloaded. Water was lapping over the side and every ripple of the current posed a danger to us. To make matters worse, the tide was going out and the strong current was sweeping us towards Silver's men on the shore.

'I cannot keep her heading towards the stockade,' I told the captain. 'Can't you row harder?'

'Not without swamping the boat,' he answered.

Suddenly Gray pointed to the ship in alarm.

'The gun!' he cried.

In our hurry, we'd completely forgotten about the ship's cannon. To our horror we could see the five pirates on board pulling the cover off the gun.

'Hands was Flint's gunner,' said Gray.

By now the current was weaker and I could steer our boat towards the stockade. But this meant we were a sitting duck for our enemies on the *Hispaniola*.

'Who's the best shot here?' asked the captain.

'Mr Trelawney by a long way,' I said.

'Mr Trelawney, will you please pick off one of those men by the gun. Hands if possible.'

Cool as steel, Trelawney raised his musket, and we stopped rowing to let him take aim. By now Hands was at the muzzle of the gun, ramming down the shot. Unluckily, just as Trelawney fired, Hands stooped down and the shot missed him. One of the other pirates fell back with a cry.

The cry was echoed by voices from the shore. Turning to look, we saw the pirates running out of the trees and scrambling into their boats.

'Here they come, sir,' said Gray.

'Row for your lives, then,' said the captain. 'It's too late to worry about swamping her now. Unless we can get ashore, we're done for.'

'Only one of the boats is coming after us,' I said. 'The others must be going round the shore to cut us off at the stockade.'

'It's not them I'm worried about,' replied the captain. 'It's the cannon.'

We were now close to shore. Thirty or forty more strokes and we'd be there. But at that moment we heard the boom of the gun and all ducked down in the boat. The shot passed just over our heads, so close that we felt the wind of it. No one was hurt, but in our haste to save ourselves we had swamped the boat. We sank in three feet of water. All our supplies were lost and, worse still, three of the five muskets we had on board.

As we waded to the beach, we could hear voices getting closer from the woods. The pirates were trying to cut us off before we could reach the stockade.

CHAPTER 18

The End of the First Day's Fighting

A strip of wood divided us from the stockade. We ran across it, hearing the pirates coming closer with every step. I could see that we would have to stand and fight.

'Captain,' I said, 'Trelawney is the best shot, give him your gun. His own is useless.'

They swapped guns and Trelawney, cool and silent, primed it ready to fire. At the same time I handed my cutlass to Gray who was unarmed. He spat in his hand and made the blade sing through the air.

We reached the edge of the wood and could see the stockade in front of us. At that moment seven of the pirates appeared, led by Job Anderson, the boatswain. When they saw we had muskets they stopped in their tracks. Before they could recover, the squire and I fired, and so did Hunter and Joyce in the log-house. The volley of shots was enough. One of the pirates fell dead to the ground while his friends turned and fled into the woods.

As we ran to the stockade a pistol shot rang out from the woods. The ball whistled past my ear, and poor Tom Redruth stumbled and fell.

We carried the gamekeeper, groaning and bleeding, to the log-house. The poor fellow was the oldest among us. The squire bent over him and kissed his hand, crying like a child.

'Be I dying, doctor?' he asked.

'Tom,' I said. 'You're going home.'

The squire still felt guilty for bringing us all on this doomed trip.

'Tom, say you forgive me,' he pleaded.

'Would that be respectful like, from me to you, squire?' asked Tom. 'So be it, amen.'

Not long after he died without a word.

The captain put a hand on the squire's shoulder. 'All's well with Tom. He died doing his duty to this captain and his master. All's well with him, never fear.'

The captain had brought two Union Jacks from the ship. He placed one over Tom's body and the other he hoisted over the stockade. Having done that, he took me on one side.

'Dr Livesey, in how many weeks do you expect the squire's friend in Bristol to send a ship to look for us?'

'It's a question of months, not weeks,' I replied. 'We agreed that he would wait until the end of August.'

The captain looked worried. 'Then it's a great pity, sir, we lost that second boat-load. We have enough ammunition to last out, but our food supplies are short. Very short.'

Suddenly there was a roar and a whistle. A cannonball passed high above our roof and landed beyond us in the wood.

'Oho!' cried the captain. 'Blaze away, lads, and use up your powder.'

The next shot landed a little closer.

'Captain,' said the squire, 'the log-house can't be seen from the ship, it's the flag they're aiming at. Wouldn't it be wiser to take it down?'

'Take down our colours?' cried the captain. 'Never, sir. We'll show those rogues we're not afraid of them.'

All through the evening the cannon kept thundering away. Ball after ball flew over or fell short, but none did any damage.

Later the captain sat down to write in the ship's log. He wrote:

> 'Captain Smollett, Dr Livesey, Squire Trelawney, Abraham Gray, John Hunter and Richard Joyce. We are all the loyal men left of the ship's company. We have stores for ten days on short rations. Thomas Redruth, owner's servant, was shot by the mutineers. James Hawkins, cabin-boy ...'

What had happened to poor Jim Hawkins? I was

wondering this myself when we heard a voice outside the stockade.

'Doctor! Squire! Captain! Hello, Hunter, is that you?'

I ran to the door to see Jim Hawkins safe and sound, climbing over the stockade.

CHAPTER 19

Jim Hawkins Takes up the Story Again

Holding the Stockade

As soon as Ben Gunn saw the flag flying over the stockade, he caught my arm.

'There's your friends, sure enough,' he said.

'Just as likely it's Silver and his mutineers,' I replied.

'No, Silver would fly the Jolly Roger!' he cried. 'Them's your friends. There's been a fight and I reckon they got the better of it. Now they're in the old stockade that Flint built years ago.'

'Then we must go and join them,' I said.

'Hold, mate,' said Ben. 'Ben is smart. I'm not going in there, not till I see your fine gentleman and has his word of honour. You tell him, Ben Gunn has reasons of his own. And when you want me you'll know where to find me. He's to come alone, mind.'

I nodded. 'I understand. You want to speak with the squire and you can be found where I met you today. Is that all?'

'That's it,' he said, still holding on to me. 'I reckon you can go, Jim. But don't forget, "Reasons of his own," says you.'

He was interrupted by a loud crack, and a cannonball came tearing through the trees a hundred yards away from where we stood. Both of us ran off in different directions.

For the next hour, balls kept crashing through the woods and I dared not go near the stockade. At last, after sunset, I crept along the shore keeping to the trees. I could see the *Hispaniola* a little way out. Sure enough, the pirates' skull and crossbones now flew from her mast. Along the beach, a fire glowed among the trees. Boats were going back and forth from the ship and the pirates' loud shouts suggested they were drunk.

I started to make a wide circle back towards the stockade. On my way I passed a white rock, high above some bushes. I guessed this was the place Ben Gunn had mentioned. Now I knew where to find a boat if I needed one in the future.

Keeping to the woods, I came up behind the stockade and was warmly welcomed by my old friends. I soon told them all about my strange meeting with Ben Gunn.

The log-house was built on top of a hill, roughly made

out of pine trunks. A spring bubbled up inside and served
as a well. Our chimney was a square hole cut in the roof.
Little smoke from the fire went out that way, so we were
always coughing and rubbing our eyes. All in all it was a
gloomy place.

Captain Smollett kept our spirits up by giving us jobs
to do. Two of us were sent to collect firewood, while two
more dug a grave for poor Tom Redruth. The doctor was
appointed cook while I was on sentry duty at the door.

Later Dr Livesey came out to speak to me. 'This man, Ben Gunn, what do you make of him, Jim?'

'I don't know, sir. After three years on this island, I think he may be a little mad.'

After supper, we discussed our situation. Things looked bleak. Our food supplies were so low that we'd be starved into surrender before help ever reached us. Our only chance was to pick off as many of the pirates as we could, until they either surrendered or ran off with the *Hispaniola*. Besides that, the doctor felt sure the pirates would be down with the fever within a week.

After all the adventures of the day I was dead tired and slept like a log.

I was woken in the morning by the sound of voices.

'A flag of truce!' someone cried. 'And it's Silver himself!'

CHAPTER 20

Silver's Offer

There were two men outside the stockade. One of them was waving a white cloth, the other was Silver himself. It was a damp, cold morning and they stood knee-deep in a white mist.

'Stay where you are, men,' said the captain. 'This could be a trick.'

He called to the pirates. 'Who goes there? Stand or we fire.'

'Flag of truce,' cried Silver.

The captain kept out of sight in the porch and spoke to us in a low voice.

'Dr Livesey, take the north side, you, Jim, the east, Gray, the west. Have your muskets loaded and keep your eyes open. Look lively now, lads.'

He turned again to the mutineers.

'What do you want?'

The other pirate replied. 'Cap'n Silver, sir, to come aboard and offer terms of peace.'

'Cap'n Silver! Don't know him! Who's he?' cried the
captain scornfully.

This time Long John answered for himself. 'Me, sir.
These poor lads have chosen me captain, after you
deserted your post, sir. We want to strike a bargain.'

'Very well,' said Smollett. 'If you wish to talk to me,
come up here.'

Silver threw his crutch over the stockade and climbed
over. He was dressed in his best blue coat with thick
brass buttons. A fine laced hat was pushed back on his
head.

He sat down on the sand. 'Well, well, here we all are
together like a happy family, you might say.'

'If you have anything to say, man, then say it,' replied the captain, curtly.

'Right you are, Cap'n Smollett,' said Silver. 'That was a clever trick of yours last night to kill a man in his sleep. But mark me, cap'n, we'll be on sentry duty next time.'

'Well?' said the captain coolly. What Silver said was a riddle to him, though you never would have guessed it.

As for me, I had an idea it was Ben Gunn who had visited the pirates last night. From what Silver said, we had one less of our enemies to deal with.

'Well, here's the long and short of it,' said Silver. 'We want that treasure and you have it. So here's my offer. You give us the chart and stop shooting poor seamen, and I'll give you a choice. You can come aboard the ship, once we have the treasure and, on my word of honour, we'll deliver you to a safe port. Or if that ain't to your fancy, you can stay here. We'll give you a share of the stores and I'll send the first ship we sight to pick you up. Now that's my offer and if it ain't handsome I don't know what is.'

'Is that all?' asked the captain, puffing on his pipe.

'Every last word, by thunder!' replied John.

'Very good,' said the captain. 'Now you listen to me. You can't find the treasure. You can't sail the ship – not a man of you can read a compass. You can't even fight us in this stockade. So here's *my* offer. If you surrender now, I'll take you home in irons and promise you a fair trial in England. If not, I'll put a bullet in your back next time I meet you. Now move, lad. On your way at the double.'

Silver's face was a picture. He glared at the captain in silent fury.

'Give me a hand up,' he growled at last.

'Not I,' said the captain.

Muttering curses, Silver crawled to the porch where he could pull himself up. Then he spat on the sand.

'There! That's what I think of you. Before the hour's out, you'll be laughing on the other side of your faces. Them that die will be the lucky ones.'

He stumped off down the hill and we watched him go.

CHAPTER 21

Attack

'My lads,' said the captain, 'within the hour we'll be under attack. We may be outnumbered, but we have the advantage of shelter. I've no doubt we can beat them if we fight like men.'

We began to make preparations.

'Doctor, you take the door and fire through the porch,' said the captain. 'Gray and Mr Trelawney, you take the north side, it's there that the danger will come from. Hunter, take the east side, Joyce cover the west. Hawkins, you and I will stand by to load the guns.'

We waited. In an hour the sun had crept above the treetops and the sand was baking hot. We stood at our posts in a fever of heat and nerves.

For a long time it was silent, till suddenly Joyce raised his musket and fired. In answer, a volley of shots came from every side of the stockade. Several bullets struck the log-house but none entered.

Seconds later the pirates burst out of the woods with a loud cry. They came from the north side, swarming over the fence like monkeys. The squire and Gray fired again and again. Three of the pirates fell to the ground, but four more had made it over the fence. They ran up the hill towards us as their friends kept up a steady fire from the trees.

I saw the head of Job Anderson, the boatswain, appear at one of the loopholes.

'At 'em, lads – at 'em!' he roared in a frenzy.

At the same time a pirate grabbed Hunter's musket through the loophole. With a stunning blow he caught Hunter on the head and laid him out on the floor. Meanwhile a third pirate appeared in the doorway and attacked the doctor with his cutlass. The log-house was so full of smoke it was hard to tell friend from enemy.

'Out, lads, out and fight them in the open. Cutlasses!' cried the captain.

I snatched a cutlass from the pile and ran outside.

In front of me the doctor chased his attacker down the hill and sent him sprawling with a slash of his blade.

Next moment I found myself face to face with Anderson. He roared and I saw his cutlass flash in the sun above his head. Just before the blow came, I leapt to one side. I lost my footing in the sand and rolled down the hill. When I looked up the attack was over. Gray had shot Anderson before he could recover.

Another pirate had been shot through a loophole. Of the four who had entered the stockade only one was left and he was clambering back out in a hurry.

Victory was ours but it had been won at a heavy cost. Back in the log-house we found Hunter lying still stunned, while Joyce had been shot through the head.

The squire was bent over the captain.

'He's wounded,' said Trelawney.

'Have they run?' asked Mr Smollett.

'All that could,' replied the doctor. 'There's five of them will never run again.'

'Five!' cried the captain. 'Well done, lads. Now it's nine of them against our four.'

CHAPTER 22

How My Sea Adventure Began

Our enemies didn't return. They'd 'got their rations for the day' as the captain put it.

It gave us time to tend our wounded and get dinner.

The squire and I cooked outside away from the loud groans coming from the doctor's patients indoors.

There wasn't much he could do for poor Hunter who died later that night. The captain lived but was badly wounded. He'd been shot twice: in the shoulder and in the leg. The doctor said he shouldn't walk nor move his arm for some weeks.

After dinner, the squire and the doctor sat talking for a while. To my surprise I saw the doctor arm himself with a musket and cutlass, put the treasure map in his pocket and climb over the stockade. Gray and I watched him as he disappeared into the trees.

'In the name of Davy Jones, is the doctor mad?' asked Gray.

'Not him,' I said. 'My guess is he's going to find Ben Gunn.'

Meanwhile there was nothing much to do but sit and

wait. Inside the stockade the sun blazed down and I began to feel sick with all the poor dead bodies lying around. How I envied the doctor walking in the cool shade of the woods! While I was washing up the dinner things I began to think of a plan. Maybe I was foolish, but I was only a boy and I didn't consider the danger.

The squire and Gray were busy helping the captain with his bandages. This was my chance. I filled my pockets with biscuits and a couple of pistols. Then, while no one was watching I made my escape over the fence and into the trees. My plan was to find the white rock and see if Ben Gunn's boat really was there. I was leaving only two fit men to guard the log-house but that couldn't be helped.

It took me all afternoon to reach the white rock, often crawling through the bushes on all fours. By the time I'd reached the place it was getting dark. Under the rock I found a little tent of goat-skins, hidden by bushes. Sure enough, beneath the tent was Ben Gunn's boat. It was a small, home-made craft, rather like a coracle. Round as a soup bowl, it was made of goat skins stretched over a wooden frame. And now I'd found the boat another bold idea entered my head. What was to stop me slipping out to the *Hispaniola* and cutting her adrift?

It was a perfect night for my plan. Black darkness had settled over Treasure Island and the night was clothed in a thick fog. There were only two points of light. One was from the cabin of the *Hispaniola* and the other was the great fire by the river where the pirates sat drinking and laughing.

The tide was already going out and I had to wade out through a belt of swampy sand. Soon I had my round boat in the water and was paddling out towards the shadow of the great ship.

CHAPTER 23

Under the Ship

The coracle floated well upon the water, but it was an awkward boat to steer.

Whatever I did, it always spun round and round in the water. If it hadn't been for the strong tide going out, I would never have reached the ship. Suddenly there she was towering above me like a great ink-blot in the darkness.

The rippling current bubbled and chattered around me. I took out my knife and began to cut the anchor rope, one strand at a time.

Above me I could hear the sound of voices from the cabin. Israel Hands and another man were quarrelling drunkenly. As I worked, a cabin window opened and one of them threw something out. An empty rum bottle

splashed into the sea not far away. On the shore I could see the red glow of the camp fire and hear one of the pirates crooning the old sea song:
'Fifteen men on the dead man's chest
Yo-ho-ho and a bottle of rum!'

With a last effort I cut through the rope. Once free, the ship began to twist and turn in the strong current. It was then I noticed the rope trailing down into the water. The opportunity to see into the cabin was too good to resist. Grabbing hold of the rope, I hauled myself up hand over hand.

When my eyes were level with the window sill, I could see Hands and the other man. They were locked together with their hands round each other's throats. Their two crimson faces swayed under the smoky lamp.

Just then the ship gave a sudden lurch and seemed to change her course. I lost my grasp on the rope and dropped down into the coracle. The current had changed. It was moving faster, bubbling and muttering. The *Hispaniola* was being swept out to sea. Worse still, I was being drawn with her!

Above me I could hear shouts and the pounding of feet. The two drunkards had at last woken up to the disaster.

There was nothing I could do but lie down in the bottom of my little boat and pray. Soon we were carried out into rough water. The coracle was tossed about like a

cork, rising and falling on huge waves. I lay there in the bottom of the boat for hours until weariness finally overcame my terror and I fell asleep.

CHAPTER 24

The Cruise of the Coracle

It was broad daylight when I woke up. I found myself about a quarter of a mile off Treasure Island. I could clearly see Haulbowline Head with its high cliffs. My first thought was to paddle to the shore. But as I drew nearer I could see it was hopeless. The cliffs were ringed with fallen rocks where the breakers crashed foaming white. If I tried to land my little boat I would be dashed to pieces.

By now the sun was higher and I began to be tortured by thirst. The seawater caked my lips with salt and my throat was burning. It was clear the current was carrying me past the island and I began to lose all hope. If I couldn't steer my boat to land, I would either starve at sea or be drowned.

Suddenly, half a mile away, I saw a sight that gave me fresh heart. It was the *Hispaniola*, under sail. I knew I'd be taken prisoner if I reached her, but by now I was so thirsty I hardly cared.

The ship was behaving oddly. One minute she would

lie idle, then the wind would fill the sails and she would set off swiftly. Up and down she went, sailing in swoops and dashes. At first I thought that the men on board were drunk but then the truth dawned on me. There was no one sailing the ship – the *Hispaniola* was deserted! I might recapture her, if I could only get on board.

For some time I paddled after her, until with luck I started to gain. I could see the cabin window at the stern hanging open and the lamp inside still burning. When I was only a hundred yards away a strong gust of wind caught the ship. She began to turn in the wind. With a shock, I realized she was heading straight for me. One minute I was below a wave, then the ship loomed above me. I had no time to think or cry out. The bowsprit was above my head. Standing in the coracle, I leapt to grab it. For a few seconds I clung there, hanging on for dear life. Below me there was a thud as my little boat was crushed beneath the ship.

CHAPTER 25

The Jolly Roger

If I stayed where I was I knew I'd be tossed into the sea. As soon as the wind dropped, I crawled along the bowsprit and fell forward onto the deck.

There was not a soul on deck, only muddy footprints and a broken bottle rolling backwards and forwards with the rise and fall of the ship.

Further on I found the two watchmen. Israel Hands was propped against the side, chalk-faced, with his jaw hanging open. His companion was stone dead. Hands gave a low moan and I walked over to look at him.

His eyes rolled towards me. 'Brandy,' was the only word he could speak.

I went below to look for a bottle and found the cabin in a terrible state. Empty bottles clinked in every corner of the rolling ship. The doctor's books lay open and half the pages had been torn out to light the mutineers' pipes. It was clear that since the mutiny had begun, not one of Silver's men had been sober.

I found a bottle of brandy, and some biscuits and cheese for myself. Then I went back to Hands. On the way I stopped to take a long, deep drink from the water barrel.

Hands took the brandy without a word and drank from it greedily.

'Ay, by thunder, I needed that,' he said.

'Are you badly hurt?' I asked.

He grunted. 'If that doctor was aboard I'd be right in no time. But I don't have no luck, see. And where did you spring from?'

'Well,' I said. 'I've come aboard to take charge of the ship. From now on, you'll treat me as your captain, Mr Hands. And to begin with I can't have this flag on my ship.'

I ran to where the black Jolly Roger was flying from the top mast. Pulling it down, I threw it overboard.

'God save the king!' I cried. 'And an end to Cap'n Silver.'

Hands watched me slyly all the time through narrow eyes.

'Well, Cap'n Hawkins, I reckon you'll be wanting to get ashore,' he said. 'So suppose we have a talk.'

'Talk away, Mr Hands,' I said and went back to my meal.

Hands nodded at the dead pirate on the deck. 'This man, O'Brien and me, we got the sail up and meant to take the ship back. Well he's dead now, so there's only you to sail her. Now look here, you gives me food and drink and ties up my wound and I'll tell you how to sail the ship. That's square all round, ain't it?'

'Agreed,' I said. 'But we're not going back to the anchorage where Silver is. I mean to bring her round the North Inlet and we'll beach her there quietly.'

'To be sure,' said Hands. 'I haven't no choice have I?'

I bandaged his wound and after he'd drunk some more of the brandy, he seemed to look more himself. With his instructions, I soon had the ship heading for the island. We raced past the coast and headed north towards the inlet.

I was in high spirits. Up to now I'd blamed myself for deserting my post at the stockade. But now I'd rescued the ship and was going back to help my friends. The sun shone and the ship skimmed before the breeze like a bird.

Only Hands spoiled my happiness. I could feel his eyes following me as I went about my work, watching me with a crafty smile on his face.

CHAPTER 26

Israel Hands

We had to wait for the tide to turn before we could sail into the inlet. We both sat in silence over another meal.

'This here's an unlucky ship, Jim,' said Hands at last. 'There's been too many poor seamen died since we took her out of Bristol. O'Brien, he's dead, ain't he? Well, do you think a dead man is dead for good, or do he come back as a ghost?'

'You can kill the body but not the spirit,' I replied.

'Maybe O'Brien is watching us now from another world.'

'Ah well, spirits don't count for much in my book,' said Hands. 'I'll chance it with the spirits, Jim. And now I'd thank you to go down below and get me a bottle of wine. This brandy's too strong for my head.'

I'd never known Hands prefer wine to brandy before. I suspected he had some reason for wanting me off the deck. He had a way of smiling and licking his lips that would have told a child he was up to something.

I went below, making plenty of noise. Then I slipped off my shoes and doubled back to the galley. There I popped my head above the ladder where I could keep an eye on Hands. Just as I suspected, he was now dragging himself across the deck. From under a coil of rope he picked up a dagger, red with blood, and hid it under his jacket. Then he crawled back to his old position to be ready for me.

Israel was armed and planning to kill me, that much was obvious. Yet I was certain he would wait until I had beached us safely on the island. The coxswain couldn't manage the ship without me.

I came back on deck with a bottle of wine. Hands smashed the neck off the bottle and took a good swig.

'Here's luck!' he said. 'Ah Jim, Jim! I'm not long for this world.'

'Then you'd better say your prayers like a Christian,' I replied.

'Why?' said he.

'Why?' I cried. 'You've joined a mutiny, you've lived by lies and blood. There's a man lying over there that you murdered. God's mercy, that's why, Mr Hands!'

I'd spoken angrily, but Israel didn't lose his temper. Instead he replied almost thoughtfully.

'I've been at sea for thirty years, and I never seen any good come out of goodness yet. Him who strikes first lives longest. Dead men don't bite. Them's my views.'

When the tide had changed we sailed into the inlet. It was a narrow passage but with Hands as pilot and me at the tiller, we made a neat job of it.

'Look, there's a fine flat bit of sand,' he called. 'Stand by to beach her. Steady! Steady!'

I was so busy with the ship that I forgot to keep a watchful eye on the coxswain. Suddenly I felt uneasy. Whirling round, I saw Hands creeping up behind me with the dagger in his hand.

He gave a roar like a charging bull and threw himself at me. I leapt aside and let go of the tiller. This probably saved my life as it swung round and struck him in the chest. I backed away and drew a pistol from my pocket. As Hands came towards me I pulled the trigger. There was no flash or sound. The powder was wet with sea water!

I was defenceless and Hands knew it. He came on,

his greasy hair tumbling across his red face. At that moment the *Hispaniola* struck the beach. The ship tipped over to one side and we both rolled down the deck. I was on my feet first and I sprang into the rigging. Quick as a monkey I climbed up, not pausing until I was sitting on the cross-trees. I lost no time in starting to reload my pistols with dry powder. Hands saw the danger and began to climb after me. He held his dagger in his teeth but made slow progress, hauling his wounded leg after him. Before he was half way up I had both my pistols ready.

I called out, 'One more step, Mr Hands, and I'll blow your brains out. Dead men don't bite, you know,' I added with a laugh.

He took his dagger from his mouth. 'Jim, as you see, I don't have no luck. I reckon we'll have to strike a bargain, you and me.'

I sat there as smug as a cock on a rooftop. All of a sudden his right hand went back and his dagger sang through the air like an arrow. I felt a sharp pain in my shoulder as it pinned me to the mast. In the shock both my pistols went off without me taking aim. With a cry Israel Hands plunged from the rigging into the sea below.

CHAPTER 27

Pieces of Eight

Far below me I could see Hands' body floating face-down in the green sea.

I began to feel sick and faint. There was blood running down my chest from my wounded shoulder. The pain was like the burning of a red hot iron. I feared that if I passed out I'd fall and join Hands in the green water below.

Once I inspected my wound I found it was less serious

than I'd thought. The dagger only held me by a pinch of skin and the cloth of my jacket. With one painful jerk, I was able to pull myself free and climb slowly down to the deck.

After I had bathed my wound, I lost no time in going ashore. The sun was setting and I could hear the breeze singing in the tossing pine trees. I waded through the shallow water, leaving the *Hispaniola* leaning on her side. I was looking forward to reaching the stockade. Imagine my friends' faces when they heard that I'd brought back the ship single-handed!

By the time I reached the stockade, the moon had climbed high. I could see a red glow in the sky. On the other side of the log-house a great fire had burned itself down to embers. I stopped in my tracks, puzzled. The captain had never let us build large fires within the stockade before. I began to fear that something was wrong.

I climbed over the tall fence and crept up the hill on my hands and knees. As I drew nearer to the log-house, I heard a sound that was music to my ears. It was the peaceful snores of my friends inside. Standing up, I entered the pitch dark room, walking with my arms out in front of me. My plan was to lie down in my place and give my friends a surprise in the morning.

Suddenly my foot struck a sleeping body. A shrill voice split the darkness.

'Pieces of eight! Pieces of eight! Pieces of eight!'

It was Silver's parrot, Captain Flint!

I had no time to recover. Silver's voice cried, 'Who goes there?'

I turned to escape but ran straight into someone who held me tight.

'Bring a torch, Dick,' said Silver. 'Let's see what we have here.'

CHAPTER 28

In the Enemy's Camp

The red glare of the torch showed me my worst fears.

The pirates had taken the log-house and its stores. Worse still, there was no sign of any prisoners. All my friends must have died in the fight.

There were six pirates left, although one of them had a blood-stained bandage round his head.

Silver himself looked paler than when I last saw him. His fine blue coat was dirty and torn.

'So here's Jim Hawkins dropped in on us, eh? Well I call that friendly,' he said.

Sitting down on a barrel, he lit his pipe.

'Now, Jim, as you're here I'll give you a piece of my mind. I've always said you're a brave lad. I wanted you to join up with us from the first and now you've got to, mate. Your friends have turned dead against you. "Ungrateful scamp," the doctor called you. You can't go back to them for they won't have you. So you'll have to join with old Cap'n Silver.'

So far so good. My friends were still alive even if they blamed me for deserting them.

'Now I ain't one for threats, Jim,' Silver went on. 'If you like the offer, join, and if you don't you're free to say no.'

I wasn't fooled by this sneering talk. I knew the threat of death hung in the air.

'Well, if I'm to choose,' I said, 'I think I have a right to know why you're here and where my friends are.'

Silver nodded. 'Yesterday morning, Mr Hawkins,' he began, 'Doctor Livesey came out with a flag of truce.

"Cap'n Silver," says he, "you're finished. The ship's gone." We looked out and by thunder, it was true. I never seen men look such a pack of fools, as we did then. Well, the doctor he wanted to bargain. So bargain we did and here we are with the stores and the log-house. As for your mates, they've run off and where I can't tell you.'

'Is that all? And now am I meant to choose?' I asked.

'Ay, Jim,' said Silver.

'Well,' I said, 'I know what you've got in mind for me. I've seen enough men die since I met you. But I've a thing or two to tell you first. Here you are in a bad way:

ship lost, treasure lost, men lost. And if you want to know who did it, it was me. It was me overheard what you were plotting the night we sighted land. It was me who cut the ship loose and killed the men you'd left on board. And it was me who brought her to a place where you'll never find her.'

I was speaking excitedly and as no one answered, I carried on.

'You don't scare me more than a fly, Silver. Kill me or spare me, as you please. But consider one thing. If you do spare me, I give you my word I'll do what I can to save your necks, when you stand before a court of law.'

I stopped, finally out of breath. The pirates were all

staring at me like sheep. Silver however was looking at me in a new way.

Suddenly a man called Morgan jumped up and drew his knife. 'I say we've heard enough from Jim Hawkins.'

Silver turned on him. 'And who are you, Tom Morgan?

Maybe you think you are captain here? By heaven, I'll teach you. If any man crosses me, he'll end up feeding the fishes like all the others.'

Morgan paused, but the others started grumbling.

'Tom's right,' said one.

'I'll be hanged if I'll be ordered about by you, John Silver,' added another.

Silver leaned forward. 'Any of you gentlemen want to cross swords with me?' he roared. 'Well I'm ready. Take a cutlass, him who dares. That boy is more man than any one of you rats in this house. And if you lay a hand on him you'll have me to deal with.'

There was a long pause. My heart was pounding away like a sledge hammer. The pirates drew back and muttered in a corner. Then, one by one, they trooped out of the log-house. One gave Silver a mock-salute.

'Asking your pardon, sir,' he said. 'We're stepping outside to talk.'

I was left alone with Silver.

'Now look here, Jim,' said Silver in a whisper. 'You're a breath away from dying, or worse, torture. They're set on getting rid of me, but I'll stand by you, Jim. When you spoke up I see you're an honest sort. I'll stand by you and you stand by me, lad. I'll save you from them cowards, if I can. But fair's fair, when the time comes you speak up for me. You save Long John from swinging at the end of a rope.'

What Silver was asking seemed hopeless to me. He was a pirate and the ringleader of the mutiny. Still, I answered, 'What I can do, I will.'

'It's a bargain,' cried Silver. 'Now understand me, Jim, I've got a brain in my head. I'm on the squire's side now. I know you've got that ship hidden somewhere safe but I don't ask no questions.'

He took a swig of brandy. 'There's trouble brewing. And talking of trouble why did the squire give me that treasure map, I wonder, Jim?'

I was so surprised I had no answer.

'Ah well,' said Silver. 'There's some reason to it, bad or good.'

And he took another deep swallow of brandy, like a man preparing for the worst.

CHAPTER 29

The Black Spot Again

Looking out through a loophole I could see the men returning to the log-house.

'Here they come,' I said.

'Let them come,' said Silver. 'I've still got a trick or two up my sleeve.'

The door opened and the five men came in. One of them came forward nervously and put something in Silver's hand.

'The black spot! I thought so,' he said. 'Why, hello! This ain't lucky. Some fool's cut this paper out of a Bible!'

'It was Dick,' said Morgan.

'Dick, was it? Then Dick better start saying his prayers,' replied Silver.

George Merry, who seemed to be the leader, spoke up. He was a tall man with yellow eyes.

'You don't fool us no more, Silver. You've had your chance and we're all likely to hang for your mistakes. You've bungled this cruise from start to finish. You let the enemy out of this trap for nothing and now you're protecting this here boy.'

'Well now, George, let's answer them points,' said Silver coolly. 'First this boy, well ain't I keeping him as a hostage? He just may be our last chance. Kill this boy and lose our only hostage? Not me, mates! And as for striking a bargain with the enemy: you lost the ship but I found the treasure. So who's the better man now?'

With those words he tossed a yellow piece of paper on the ground. The pirates leapt on it like cats on a mouse. It passed from hand to hand and you would have thought the fools were touching the gold itself.

'That's Flint's treasure map as I live,' said one. 'There's his mark, J.F.'

'Mighty pretty,' said George. 'But how are we to get away without a ship?'

Silver sprang up. 'One more word of your sauce, George, and I'll cut you down. Now, mates, choose who you want as captain.'

'Silver!' the pirates cried. 'Barbecue for ever!'

'So that's the tune, is it?' said Silver. 'I reckon you'll have to wait another day to become captain, George. And now, shipmates, this black spot ain't worth much is it? Dick has spoiled his Bible and brought himself bad luck, that's all.'

And that was the end of the matter. Silver was too clever for his simple-minded crew. After drinks all round they went to sleep. As I closed my eyes I thought of the dangerous game Long John was playing to save his own miserable neck. Wicked as he was, I almost felt sorry for him.

CHAPTER 30

A Promise Kept

I was woken up by a loud, cheerful voice.

'Log-house ahoy!' it cried. 'The doctor is here.'

It was Dr Livesey himself come to check on his patients. I was very glad to see him, though a little ashamed to look him in the face. Silver welcomed him over the stockade.

'Top of the morning to you, sir. We've quite a surprise for you. We've a new visitor here.'

'Not Jim?'

'The same Jim as ever,' replied Silver.

The doctor stopped and for some seconds seemed unable to speak. A moment later he entered the house and gave a grim nod to me. He moved among his patients for the next hour, tending their wounds and fever. They took their medicines humbly, more like school children than bloodthirsty pirates.

'Well then, that's done for today,' the doctor said at last. 'And now I should like to have a talk with that boy, please.'

George Merry sprang to his feet. 'No!' he bellowed.

'Silence!' roared Silver, striking a barrel with his fist.

He turned to me.

'Hawkins, do you give your word of honour that you won't try to escape?'

I gave my promise.

'Then, doctor,' said Silver, 'you step outside the stockade and Jim can come down and speak to you through the fence.'

The men didn't trust this arrangement and it took all Silver's cunning to persuade them. They accused him of double-dealing, which of course was the truth.

We walked down the hill to where the doctor was waiting. Silver looked a changed man away from his friends. His cheeks seemed to have sunk in and his voice trembled slightly.

'Doctor, the boy will tell you how I saved his life last night and risked mine into the bargain. Now when a man's sailing as close to the wind as me he needs a bit of hope to go on.'

'Why, John, you're not afraid, are you?' asked Dr Livesey.

'I'm no coward, not I. But I'll own up that thinking of the gallows gives me the shakes. Doctor, you're a good man and you won't forget what I've done.'

He stepped back a little way and left the doctor and me to talk alone.

'So, Jim,' said the doctor sadly. 'Heaven knows, I don't blame you, but when Captain Smollett was well you wouldn't have dared run off like that. To run away when he was wounded was a cowardly act.'

I blinked back the tears in my eyes. 'Doctor, I have already blamed myself enough,' I said. 'I'd be dead by now if it wasn't for Silver. And I was willing to die. It's the torture that I'm afraid of. If they find out …'

'Jim!' the doctor interrupted. 'Jim, I can't leave you with these scoundrels. Jump over this fence and we'll run for it together.'

'No,' I replied. 'I gave my word. Silver trusted me and I can't break my promise. But let me finish. If they torture me, I might tell them where I have beached the ship …'

'The ship?' cried the doctor in amazement. 'You have the ship?'

He listened in silence as I told him the story of my adventures at sea. When I'd finished he shook his head in admiration.

'All along it's been you that has saved our lives, Jim,' he said. 'You discovered the plot, you found Ben Gunn and now you have brought back the ship.'

He called Long John over. 'Silver, I'll give you one piece of advice. Don't be in any hurry to find that treasure.'

'Why?' asked Silver. 'I can only save my own neck and the boy's by looking for the treasure. Now speak honest with me, doctor: why did you leave the stockade and give me that treasure map?'

The doctor shook his head. 'The secret isn't mine to tell,' he said. 'But I'll tell you this much. If we ever get out of this man-trap alive, I'll do my best to save you. Keep the boy close to you and when you need help, call for it. Goodbye, Jim.'

The doctor shook hands with me and strode off back into the wood.

CHAPTER 31

The Treasure Hunt

'Jim,' said Silver when we were alone, 'I heard the doctor begging you to make a run for it. And I heard you say no plain as day. Jim, I saved your life and now you saved mine. I won't forget it. And now we're to go in for treasure hunting. You and me must stick close together, Jim.'

During breakfast, Silver kept talking all the time. 'Ay, mates,' he said. 'It's lucky you've got Long John to think for you. They have the ship right enough. Where they hid it I don't know yet, but once we've got the treasure we'll have to look lively and find it.'

In this way he kept the men's spirits up. I myself was too anxious to feel hungry. I still didn't know whether to trust Silver. Whose side was he on? It was certain that if the pirates knew the game he was playing they'd kill him and me on the spot. Added to that, why had the doctor given Silver the treasure map? And what had he meant about expecting trouble? These questions went round and round my head.

Everyone but me was armed to the teeth. Silver carried two muskets, as well as a cutlass and pistols in his pockets. He had a rope tied round my waist and led me along like a dancing bear.

We went down to the beach and paddled the boats up the river towards Spy Glass Hill. Flint's map told us to look for a tall tree on Spy Glass Shoulder. When we reached the brow of the hill we could see a dozen tall trees above us. The men spread out to search, running and leaping excitedly. Suddenly there was a terrified cry from one of them.

We hurried to the spot. Lying under a big pine tree was a human skeleton. The grim sight struck a chill to every heart.

'What sort of way is that for bones to lie?' said George Merry. 'It ain't natural.'

The skeleton lay perfectly straight with its hands raised above its head like a diver.

'There's our compass,' said Silver. 'This here's a pointer, showing us the way to go. By thunder, it turns my blood cold to think of Flint. This is one of his jokes and no mistake. He came ashore with six men and killed every one of them. Then he hauled these bones up here and laid them down to point the way.'

He gave a shudder. 'It's lucky Flint ain't living. There were six of them and there's six of us now.'

'I saw Flint dead myself,' said Morgan. 'They buried him with penny pieces on his eyes.'

'Dead sure enough,' said another. 'But if ever a ghost walked, it would be Flint's.'

'Come, come,' said Silver. 'He's dead and he won't walk. Let's on and find the treasure.'

We went on but all the eagerness had gone out of the pirates. Now they talked in low voices and kept close together.

CHAPTER 32

The Voice Among the Trees

The climb was steep and after a while we sat down to rest. Ever since the skeleton, the men's voices had dropped almost to a whisper.

'I don't feel sharp,' said Morgan. 'It's thinking of Flint that's done it.'

'He were an ugly devil, blue in the face,' said Merry.

All of a sudden, a thin trembling voice started to sing from somewhere in the trees:
'Fifteen men on the dead man's chest
Yo-ho-ho and a bottle of rum!'

The pirates were struck dumb with fear. Some of them caught hold of each other. Morgan grovelled on the ground.

'It's Flint!' he gasped.

The song had stopped as soon as it had started.

'Come,' said Silver. 'It can't be Flint. It's someone playing games with us. Someone flesh and blood.'

The pirates still didn't move. Then the voice came again, not singing, but wailing.

'Darby M'Graw! Darby M'Graw! Fetch the rum, Darby!'

The pirates looked at each other, startled.

'That fixes it,' moaned Morgan. 'Them were Flint's last words.'

'Let's go,' urged another. Dick had his Bible out and was praying under his breath.

Still Silver wouldn't give in. 'Nobody on this island knew about Darby but us,' he said. 'But shipmates, I'm here to get that treasure. I never feared Flint when he was alive and I'll face him dead now if I have to. There's seven hundred thousand pound buried up ahead and Silver's not the man to leave it there.'

I think the men would have run away if they'd dared. Instead they kept close to Silver who was thinking hard. Suddenly his face lit up. 'By the powers, I have it. That voice was no ghost. When did a ghost ever have an echo? It's a trick. That voice is Ben Gunn's.'

Morgan got off his knees. 'Ay, so it were. Ben Gunn!'

'Why, nobody's afraid of Ben Gunn, dead or alive,' cried Merry.

Soon we had set off again for Spy Glass Hill. The men had got over their fright and were now chatting together. Only Dick held tight to his Bible.

On the shoulder of the hill we found three trees. The

third was a giant, with a red trunk taller than a ship's mast. Somewhere in its great shadow was the spot where Flint's treasure lay buried. The men ran ahead towards it. Silver hobbled after them, pulling me roughly along behind. Whenever I stumbled he gave me an evil look. With the gold in his sights, it was clear what he had in mind. He meant to seize the treasure, find the *Hispaniola* and cut every honest throat on the island.

Ten yards in front of us the men suddenly stopped. In a few moments we were up with them and could see why.

In front of us was a large hole. At the bottom was a broken spade and a few pieces of broken packing cases. One of the planks bore the name *Walrus* – the name of Flint's ship.

Someone had got to the treasure before us. The seven hundred thousand pounds were gone!

CHAPTER 33

The Fall of a Captain

Each of the six men stared into the pit, thunderstruck. But Silver didn't waste his time on regret. He had changed his plans before the others had time to get over the shock.

He handed me a pistol and muttered: 'Jim, take that, and stand by for trouble.'

'So you've changed sides again,' I whispered back with a look of disgust.

The pirates were leaping into the pit with cries and curses. They dug with their bare hands in the dirt. George Merry found one gold coin and held it up to Silver.

'That's your seven hundred thousands pounds, is it? Oh, a fine bargain you made!'

'Dig away, boys,' said Silver with a hollow laugh.

'Hear that, mates?' roared Merry. 'He knew there was no treasure all along. You can see it written on his face.'

'Standing for captain again, Merry?' asked Silver.

The mutineers scrambled out of the pit. There we stood, five on one side and two on the other and the pit between us. Silver never moved. He watched them as cool-headed as ever.

At last Merry spoke. 'There's only two of them. One's that one-legged cripple and the other's no more than a boy. Now, mates ...'

He was raising his arm, about to charge when – crack! crack! crack! Three musket shots came from the bushes. Merry tumbled forward into the pit and the pirate with the bandaged head fell down dead. The other three ran for their lives.

At the same moment Dr Livesey, Gray and Ben Gunn burst out of the trees. 'Forward!' cried the doctor. 'Cut them off before they reach the boats!'

We set off running, but the mutineers were not running for the boats. They fled into the woods to avoid a fight.

'Thank you kindly, doctor,' said Silver when he caught up. 'I reckon you came in about the nick of time for me and Jim. And so it *was* you, Ben Gunn. You're a nice one, to be sure.'

Ben Gunn wriggled and grinned. 'How do you do, Mr Silver? Pretty well, thank you, says you.'

As we walked down to the boats, the doctor told us the whole story. Ben Gunn had found Flint's treasure months before we arrived on the island. He dug it up and hid it in the cave where he'd made his home.

When Dr Livesey heard this he realized the treasure map was useless. The next day he'd offered Silver the map along with the stockade and its stores. In return he and his friends were allowed to leave in safety. They moved camp to Ben Gunn's cave where they could guard the treasure. That morning they'd waited in ambush for us to arrive. It was Ben Gunn who had played on the pirates' fears of Flint's ghost.

Our next thought was to find the *Hispaniola*. When we reached the inlet we found the tide had lifted her off the beach, but luckily she hadn't drifted far. Soon we were sailing for Rum Cove and Ben Gunn's cave.

At the cave we met the squire waiting for us. He

greeted me warmly but was taken aback by Silver's polite salute.

'John Silver,' he said. 'You are a villain and a liar, but the doctor tells me you saved Jim's life. Very well then, I won't hand you over to the law, but the dead men, sir, hang about your neck like millstones.'

'Thank you kindly, sir,' replied Silver with another salute.

Gunn's cave was a large one with a spring of clear water at the back. In a far corner I could see piles of coins and mountains of gold bars. At last I was looking at Flint's treasure that we'd come so far to find. It had cost the lives of seventeen men who had sailed on the *Hispaniola*. How many more lives, what blood and sorrow, what sunken ships, lies and cruelty, I couldn't tell. But the only men of Flint's crew left to see it were Silver and poor half-crazed Ben Gunn.

Captain Smollett was lying by a fire. Raising himself on his elbow, he said, 'Is that you, John Silver? What are you doing here?'

'Come back to do my duty, sir,' answered Silver.

Later we all ate a hearty meal. Silver sat with us, joining in the laughter and springing up when anything was wanted. For all the world he seemed like the same humble, cheerful cook who had sailed with us from Bristol.

CHAPTER 34

Going Home

The next morning we started work early. The treasure had to be carried a mile down to the beach and then out to the *Hispaniola* by boat. It was a heavy job for so few workmen.

I was kept busy all day in the cave, packing the money into bags. I had never seen so many strange coins from every corner of the world. It was like running my hands through autumn leaves.

The work went on for days and all the time we saw nothing of the three surviving mutineers. On the third night Silver, the doctor and I were out walking when we heard wild cries coming from the woods.

'Heaven help us, it's them!' said the doctor, shaking his head sadly.

'All drunk, sir,' said Silver.

'Or raving with the fever,' said the doctor. 'If I was sure of that I would go and help them.'

'Asking your pardon, sir, that would be a mistake,' said Silver. 'Them men couldn't keep their word, not if they wanted to.'

The doctor gave him a look of contempt. 'Ay, you're the man to keep your word, Silver, we all know that.'

Silver bore such insults without complaining. Everyone treated him like a dog, apart from Ben Gunn and me. In a way, I should have thought worse of him than anyone else. I was the only one who knew how close he had come to betraying us a second time.

At last we weighed anchor and sailed out of the North Inlet. The Union Jack which had flown from the stockade now fluttered from the mast-head. As we rounded the point, we saw the three mutineers run down to the beach. They made a pitiful sight, kneeling on the sand begging

for mercy. It seemed cruel to leave them there but we could not risk another mutiny.

They continued to call out to us to have pity as we sailed by. When we didn't turn back, one of them raised a musket and fired. The shot whistled just over Silver's head and was maybe meant for him.

By noon, Spy Glass Hill had sunk out of sight. It was with great relief that I saw the last of Treasure Island.

After many days at sea we reached a port in Spanish America. The doctor, the squire and I went ashore. At the port we met a captain of an English warship who invited us to dine on his ship. It was dawn before we arrived back at the *Hispaniola* and found a shock in store for us. Silver had gone! He had escaped in a boat some hours before. The scoundrel hadn't gone empty-handed either. He'd broken into one of the sacks of coins and made off with three or four hundred guineas. None of us was sorry: we felt we were rid of him cheaply.

With a fresh crew on board we arrived home in Bristol just as Mr Blandly was thinking of sending a ship to look for us.

We all got our fair share of the treasure and spent it wisely or foolishly. Captain Smollett is now retired from the sea. Ben Gunn got a thousand pounds which he spent in less than three weeks. He lives in the country now and sings in the church choir on Sundays. We heard nothing more of Long John Silver. That cunning, one-legged pirate disappeared out of my life for ever. Maybe he lives in comfort somewhere in this world. Heaven knows he has little chance of comfort in the next.

The rest of Flint's treasure – the silver bars – still lies buried on the island as far as I know. And for all I care it can stay there. Wild horses wouldn't drag me back to Treasure Island. Sometimes in my worst dreams I hear the boom of the surf upon the beach. Or I wake up with the shrill voice of Silver's parrot, Captain Flint, ringing in my ears: 'Pieces of eight! Pieces of eight!'

Glossary

anchorage a place for a ship to drop anchor

boatswain the crew-member in change of sails and rigging

bows the front of a ship

bowsprit a thick wooden pole that sticks out at the front of the ship

broadside a direct attack by cannon

capstan a thick post which is turned to raise or lower the anchor

coracle a small round boat

coxswain the crew-member in charge of steering the boat

cross-trees heavy wooden poles at the top of a mast

customs men law officers who control goods entering or leaving the country

doubloon an old Spanish coin

fathom a unit used to measure depth of water (one fathom = six feet)

galley a ship's kitchen

golden guinea a gold coin used in past times worth £1.05

Jolly Roger the pirates' flag – the skull and crossbones

marooned left on a remote island as a punishment

mutiny when the crew takes control of the ship from the captain

oilcloth cloth made waterproof with oil

ramming down the shot using a ramrod to push the ball down inside the cannon

stern the back of a ship

stroke a blood clot in the brain that causes paralysis

swabs an insult used by sailors (a swab is a mop)

weighed anchor took up the anchor